ACCLAIM FOR

CARLOS CASTANEDA

AND HIS

POWERFUL NARRATIVE WRITINGS

"One can't exaggerate the significance of what Castaneda has done." —*The New York Times*

"Castaneda has become one of the godfathers of the New Age movement. . . . He is addressing the central issues of our time."

—*Los Angeles Times Book Review*

"It's impossible to view the world in quite the same way after reading him. . . ." —*Chicago Tribune*

"Castaneda writes well and is especially gifted in writing clearly about abstract ideas."

—*Milwaukee Journal*

"The mysteries shimmering behind the words will haunt you . . . consistently vivid, precise, and powerful." —*Chicago Daily News*

"Hypnotic reading." —*Time*

**MORE THAN SEVEN MILLION
CARLOS CASTANEDA BOOKS IN PRINT!**

Other books by Carlos Castaneda

The Teachings of Don Juan

A Separate Reality

Journey to Ixtlan

Tales of Power

The Second Ring of Power

The Eagle's Gift

The Fire from Within

The Power of Silence

The Art of Dreaming

Magical Passes

The Active Side of Infinity

CARLOS CASTANEDA

THE WHEEL OF TIME

THE SHAMANS OF ANCIENT MEXICO,
THEIR THOUGHTS ABOUT LIFE,
DEATH AND THE UNIVERSE

WASHINGTON SQUARE PRESS
PUBLISHED BY POCKET BOOKS

New York   London   Toronto   Sydney

The Author is grateful to:

University of California Press for permission to reprint excerpts and paraphrasings from *The Teachings of Don Juan: A Yaqui Way of Knowledge,* © 1968, all rights reserved.

Simon & Schuster, Inc. for permission to reprint excerpts and paraphrasings from: *A Separate Reality: Further Conversations with Don Juan,* © 1971; *Journey to Ixtlan: The Lessons of Don Juan,* © 1972; *Tales of Power,* © 1974; *The Second Ring of Power,* © 1977; *The Eagle's Gift,* © 1981; *The Fire from Within,* © 1984; *The Power of Silence: Further Lessons of Don Juan,* © 1987; all rights reserved.

and to HarperCollins Publishers, Inc.

A Washington Square Press Publication of
POCKET BOOKS, a division of Simon & Schuster, Inc.
1230 Avenue of the Americas, New York, NY 10020

ISBN: 0-7434-1280-X

First Washington Square Press trade paperback printing January 2001

10 9 8

WASHINGTON SQUARE PRESS and colophon are registered trademarks of Simon & Schuster, Inc.

Cover design by Brigid Pearson
Front cover illustration by Marc Burckhardt

Printed in the U.S.A.

CONTENTS

CONTENTS

THE
WHEEL
OF TIME

Introduction

This series of specially selected quotations was gathered from the first eight books that I wrote about the world of the shamans of ancient Mexico. The quotations were taken directly from the explanations given to me as an anthropologist by my teacher and mentor don Juan Matus, a Yaqui Indian shaman from Mexico. He belonged to a lineage of shamans that traced its origins all the way back to the shamans who lived in Mexico in ancient times.

In the most effective manner he could afford, don Juan Matus ushered me into his world, which was, naturally, the world of those shamans of antiquity. Don Juan was, therefore, in a key position. He knew about the existence of another realm of reality, a realm which was neither illusory, nor the product of outbursts of fantasy. For don Juan and the rest of his shaman-companions—there were fifteen of them—the world of the shamans of antiquity was as real and as pragmatic as anything could be.

This work started as a very simple attempt to collect a series of vignettes, sayings, and ideas from the lore of those shamans that would be interesting to read and think about. But once the work was in progress, an unforeseeable twist of direction took place: I realized that the quotations by themselves were imbued with an extraordinary impetus. They revealed a covert train of thought that had never been evident to me before. They were pointing out the direction that don Juan's explanations had taken over the thirteen years in which he guided me as an apprentice.

Better than any type of conceptualization, the quotations revealed an unsuspected and unwavering line of action that don Juan had followed in order to promote and facilitate my entrance into his world. It became something beyond a speculation to me that if don Juan had followed that line, this must have also been the way in which his own teacher had propelled him into the world of shamans.

Don Juan Matus's line of action was his intentional attempt to pull me into what he said was another *cognitive system*. By *cognitive system*, he meant the standard definition of *cognition*: "the processes responsible for the awareness of everyday life, processes which include memory, experience, perception, and the expert use of any given syntax." Don Juan's claim was that the shamans of ancient Mexico had indeed a different cognitive system than the average man's.

Following all the logic and reasoning available to me as a student of the social sciences, I had to reject his statement. I pointed out to don Juan time and time again that whatever he was claiming was preposterous. It was, to me, an intellectual aberration at best.

It took thirteen years of hard labor on his part and on mine to discombobulate my trust in the normal system of cognition that makes the world around us comprehensible to us. This maneuver pushed me into a very strange state: a state of quasi-distrust in the otherwise implicit acceptance of the cognitive processes of our daily world.

After thirteen years of heavy onslaughts, I realized, against my very will, that don Juan Matus was indeed proceeding from another point of view. Therefore, the shamans of ancient Mexico must have had another system of cognition. To admit this burned my very being. I felt like a traitor. I felt as if I were voicing the most horrendous heresy.

When he felt that he had overcome my worst resistance, don Juan drove his point as far and as deep as he could into me, and I had to admit, without reservations, that in the world of shamans, shaman practitioners judged the world from points of view which were indescribable to our conceptualization devices. For instance, they perceived energy as it flowed freely in the universe, energy free from the bindings of socialization and syntax, pure vibratory energy. They called this act *seeing*.

Don Juan's prime objective was to help me to perceive energy as it flows in the universe. In the world of shamans, to perceive energy in such a manner is the first mandatory step toward a more engulfing, freer view of a different cognitive system. In order to elicit a *seeing* response in me, don Juan utilized other foreign units of cognition. One of the most important units, he called the *recapitulation*, which consisted of a systematic scrutiny of one's life, segment by segment, an examination made not in the light of criticism or finding flaw, but in the light of an effort to understand one's life, and to change its course. Don Juan's claim was that once any practitioner has viewed his life in the detached manner that the recapitulation requires, there's no way to go back to the same life.

To *see* energy as it flows in the universe meant, to don Juan, the capacity to *see* a human being as a *luminous egg* or *luminous ball* of energy, and to be able to distinguish, in that luminous ball of energy, certain features shared by men in common, such as a point of brilliance in the already brilliant luminous ball of energy. The claim of shamans was that it was on that point of brilliance, which those shamans called the *assemblage point*, that perception was assembled. They could extend this thought logically to mean that it was on that point of brilliance that our cognition of the world was manufactured. Odd as it may seem, don Juan Matus was right, in the sense that this is exactly what happens.

The perception of shamans, therefore, was subject to a different process than the perception of average men. Shamans claimed that perceiving energy directly led them to what they called *energetic facts*. By *energetic fact*, they meant a view obtained by *seeing* energy directly that led to conclusions that were final and irreducible; they couldn't be tampered with by speculation, or by trying to fit them into our standard system of interpretation.

Don Juan said that for the shamans of his lineage, it was an *energetic fact* that the world around us is defined by the processes of cognition, and those processes are not unalterable; they are not givens. They are a matter of training, a matter of practicality and usage. This thought was extended further, to another *energetic fact:* the processes of standard cognition are the product of our upbringing, no more than that.

Don Juan Matus knew, beyond the shadow of a doubt, that whatever he was telling me about the cognitive system of the shamans of ancient Mexico was a reality. Don Juan was, among other things, a *nagual*, which meant, for shaman practitioners, a natural leader, a person who was capable of viewing *energetic facts* without detriment to his well-being. He was, therefore, capacitated to lead his fellow men successfully into avenues of thought and perception impossible to describe.

Considering all the facts that don Juan had taught me about his cognitive world, I arrived at the conclusion, which was the conclusion that he himself shared, that the most important unit of such a world was the idea of *intent*. For the shamans of ancient Mexico, *intent* was a force they could visualize when they *saw* energy as it flows in the universe. They considered it an all-pervasive force that intervened in every aspect of time and space. It was the impetus behind everything; but what was of inconceivable value to those shamans was that *intent*—a pure abstraction—was intimately attached to man. Man could always manipulate it. The shamans of ancient Mexico realized that the only way to affect this force was through impeccable behavior. Only the most disciplined practitioner could attempt this feat.

Another stupendous unit of that strange cognitive system was the shamans' understanding and usage of the concepts of time and space. For them, time and space were not the same phenomena that form part of our lives by virtue of being an integral part of our normal cognitive system. For the average man, the standard definition of *time* is "a nonspatial continuum in which events occur in apparently irreversible succession from the past through the present to the future." And *space* is defined as "the infinite extension of the three-dimensional field in which stars and galaxies exist; the universe."

For the shamans of ancient Mexico, time was something like a thought; a thought thought by something unrealizable in its magnitude. The logical argument for them was that man, being part of that thought which was thought by forces inconceivable to his mentality, still retained a small percentage of that thought; a percentage which under certain circumstances of extraordinary discipline could be redeemed.

Space was, for those shamans, an abstract realm of activity. They called it *infinity*, and referred to it as the sum total of all the endeavors of living creatures. Space was, for them, more accessible, something almost down-to-earth. It was as if they had a bigger percentage in the abstract formulation of space. According to the versions given by don Juan, the shamans of ancient Mexico never regarded time and space as obscure abstracts the way we do. For them, both time and space, although incomprehensible in their formulations, were an integral part of man.

Those shamans had another cognitive unit called the *wheel of time*. The way they explained the *wheel of time* was to say that time was like a tunnel of infinite length and width, a tunnel with reflective furrows. Every furrow was infinite, and there were infinite numbers of them. Living creatures were compulsorily made, by the force of life, to gaze into one furrow. To gaze into one furrow alone meant to be trapped by it, to live that furrow.

A warrior's final aim is to focus, through an act of profound discipline, his unwavering attention on the *wheel of time* in order to make it turn. Warriors who have succeeded in turning the *wheel of time* can gaze into any furrow and draw from it whatever they desire. To be free from the spellbinding force of gazing into only one of those furrows means that warriors can look in either direction: as time retreats or as it advances on them.

Viewed in this manner, the *wheel of time* is an overpowering influence which reaches through the life of the warrior and beyond, as is the case with the quotations of this book. They seem to be strung together by a coil that has a life of its own. That coil, explained by the cognition of shamans, is the *wheel of time*.

Under the impact of the *wheel of time*, the aim of this book became, then, something that had not been part of the original plan. The quotations became the ruling factor, by themselves and in themselves, and the drive imposed on me by them was one of staying as close as I possibly could to the spirit in which the quotations were given. They were given in the spirit of frugality and ultimate directness.

Another thing that I tried unsuccessfully to do with the quotations was to organize them into a series of categories that would make reading them easier. However, the categorization of the quotations became untenable. There was no way of setting arbitrary categories of meaning that suited me personally to something so amorphous, so vast as a total cognitive world.

The only thing that could be done was to follow the quotations, and let them create a sketch of the skeletal form of the thoughts and feelings that the shamans of ancient Mexico had about life, death, the universe, energy. They are reflections of how those shamans understood not only the universe, but the processes of living and coexisting in our world. And more important yet, they point out the possibility of handling two systems of cognition at once without any detriment to the self.

QUOTATIONS FROM
THE TEACHINGS OF DON JUAN

Power rests on the kind of knowledge that one holds. What is the sense of knowing things that are useless? They will not prepare us for our unavoidable encounter with the unknown.

Nothing in this world is a gift. Whatever has to be learned must be learned the hard way.

A man goes to knowledge as he goes to war: wide-awake, with fear, with respect, and with absolute assurance. Going to knowledge or going to war in any other manner is a mistake, and whoever makes it might never live to regret it.

When a man has fulfilled all four of these requisites to be wide awake, to have fear, respect, and absolute assurance—there are no mistakes for which he will have to account; under such conditions his actions lose the blundering quality of the acts of a fool. If such a man fails, or suffers a defeat, he will have lost only a battle, and there will be no pitiful regrets over that.

Dwelling upon the self too much produces a terrible fatigue. A man in that position is deaf and blind to everything else. The fatigue itself makes him cease to see the marvels all around him.

Every time a man sets himself to learn, he has to labor as hard as anyone can, and the limits of his learning are determined by his own nature. Therefore, there is no point in talking about knowledge. Fear of knowledge is natural; all of us experience it, and there is nothing we can do about it. But no matter how frightening learning is, it is more terrible to think of a man without knowledge.

To be angry at people means that one considers their acts to be important. It is imperative to cease to feel that way. The acts of men cannot be important enough to offset our only viable alternative: our unchangeable encounter with infinity.

Anything is one of a million paths. Therefore, a warrior must always keep in mind that a path is only a path; if he feels that he should not follow it, he must not stay with it under any conditions. His decision to keep on that path or to leave it must be free of fear or ambition. He must look at every path closely and deliberately. There is a question that a warrior has to ask, mandatorily: Does this path have a heart?

All paths are the same: they lead nowhere. However, a path without a heart is never enjoyable. On the other hand, a path with heart is easy—it does not make a warrior work at liking it; it makes for a joyful journey; as long as a man follows it, he is one with it.

There is a world of happiness where there is no difference between things because there is no one there to ask about the difference. But that is not the world of men. Some men have the vanity to believe that they live in two worlds, but that is only their vanity. There is but one single world for us. We are men, and must follow the world of men contentedly.

A man has four natural enemies: fear, clarity, power, and old age. Fear, clarity, and power can be overcome, but not old age. Its effect can be postponed, but it can never be overcome.

Commentary

The essence of whatever don Juan said at the beginning of my apprenticeship is encapsulated in the abstract nature of the quotations selected from the first book, *The Teachings of Don Juan*. At the time of the events described in that book, don Juan spoke a great deal about *allies*, power plants, Mescalito, the little smoke, the wind, the spirits of rivers and mountains, the spirit of the chaparral, etc., etc. Later on when I questioned him about his emphasis on those elements, and why he wasn't using them anymore, he admitted unabashedly that at the beginning of my apprenticeship, he had gone into all that pseudo-Indian shaman rigmarole for my benefit.

I was flabbergasted. I wondered how he could make such a statement, which was obviously not true. He had really meant what he said about those elements of his world, and I was certainly the man who could attest to the veracity of his words and moods.

"Don't take it so seriously," he said, laughing. "It was very enjoyable for me to get into all that crap, and it was even more enjoyable because I knew that I was doing it for your benefit."

"For my benefit, don Juan? What kind of aberration is this?"

"Yes, for your benefit. I tricked you by holding your attention on items of your world which held a profound fascination for you, and you swallowed it hook, line and sinker.

"All I needed was to get your undivided attention. But how could I have done that when you had such an undisciplined spirit? You yourself told me time and time again that you stayed with me because you found what I said about the world fascinating. What you didn't know how to express was that the fascination that you felt was based on the fact that you vaguely recognized every element I was talking about. You thought that the vagueness was, of course, shamanism, and you went for it, meaning you stayed."

"Do you do this to everybody, don Juan?"

"Not to everybody, because not everybody comes to me, and above all, I'm not interested in everybody. I was and I am interested in you, you alone. My teacher, the nagual Julian, tricked me in a similar way. He tricked me with my sensuality and greed. He promised to get me all the beautiful women who surrounded him, and he promised to cover me with gold. He promised me a fortune, and I fell for it. All the shamans of my lineage had been tricked that way, since time immemorial. The shamans of my lineage are not teachers or gurus. They don't give a fig about teaching their knowledge. They want heirs to their knowledge, not people vaguely interested in their knowledge for intellectual reasons."

Don Juan was right when he said that I had fallen for his maneuver fully. I did believe that I had found the perfect shaman anthropological informant. This was the time when, under don Juan's auspices, and due to his influence, I wrote diaries and collected old maps that showed the locations of the Yaqui Indian towns throughout the centuries, beginning with the chronicles of the Jesuits in the late 1700's. I recorded all those locations and I identified the most subtle changes, and began to ponder and wonder why the towns were shifted to other locales, and why they were arranged in slightly different patterns every time they were relocated. Pseudo-speculations about reason, and reasonable doubts overwhelmed me. I collected thousands of sheets of abbreviated notes and possibilities, drawn from books and chronicles. I was a perfect student of anthropology. Don Juan spurred my fancy in every way he possibly could.

"There are no volunteers on the warriors' path," don Juan said to me under the guise of an explanation. "A man has to be forced into the warriors' path against his will."

"What do I do, don Juan, with the thousands of notes that you tricked me into collecting?" I asked him at the time.

His answer was a direct shock to me.

"Write a book about them!" he said. "I am sure that if you begin to write it, you'll never make use of those notes, anyway. They are useless, but who am I to tell you that? Find out for yourself. But don't endeavor to write a book as a writer. Endeavor to do it as a warrior, as a shaman-warrior."

"What do you mean by that, don Juan?"

"I don't know. Find it out for yourself."

He was absolutely right. I never used those notes. Instead I found myself writing unwittingly about the inconceivable possibilities of the existence of another system of cognition.

QUOTATIONS FROM
A SEPARATE REALITY

A warrior knows that he is only a man. His only regret is that his life is so short that he can't grab onto all the things that he would like to. But for him, this is not an issue; it's only a pity.

Feeling important makes one heavy, clumsy and vain. To be a warrior one needs to be light and fluid.

When they are *seen* as fields of energy, human beings appear to be like fibers of light, like white cobwebs, very fine threads that circulate from the head to the toes. Thus to the eye of a seer, a man looks like an egg of circulating fibers. And his arms and legs are like luminous bristles, bursting out in all directions.

The seer *sees* that every man is in
touch with everything else, not through
his hands, but through a bunch of long
fibers that shoot out in all directions from
the center of his abdomen. Those fibers
join a man to his surroundings; they
keep his balance; they give him stability.

When a warrior learns to *see* he *sees* that a man is a luminous egg whether he's a beggar or a king, and that there's no way to change anything; or rather, what could be changed in that luminous egg? What?

A warrior never worries about his fear. Instead, he thinks about the wonders of *seeing* the flow of energy! The rest is frills, unimportant frills.

Only a crackpot would undertake the task of becoming a man of knowledge of his own accord. A sober-headed man has to be tricked into doing it. There are scores of people who would gladly undertake the task, but those don't count. They are usually cracked. They are like gourds that look fine from the outside and yet they would leak the minute you put pressure on them, the minute you filled them with water.

When a man is not concerned with *seeing*, things look very much the same to him every time he looks at the world. When he learns to *see*, on the other hand, nothing is ever the same every time he *sees* it, and yet it is the same. To the eye of a seer, a man is like an egg. Every time he *sees* the same man he *sees* a luminous egg, yet it is not the same luminous egg.

The shamans of ancient Mexico gave the name *allies* to inexplicable forces that acted upon them. They called them *allies* because they thought they could use them to their hearts' content, a notion that proved nearly fatal to those shamans, because what they called an *ally* is a being without corporeal essence that exists in the universe. Modern-day shamans call them *inorganic beings*.

To ask what function the *allies* have is like asking what we men do in the world. We are here, that's all. And the *allies* are here like us; and maybe they were here before us.

The most effective way to live is as a warrior. A warrior may worry and think before making any decision, but once he makes it, he goes on his way, free from worries or thoughts; there will be a million other decisions still awaiting him. That's the warriors' way.

A warrior thinks of his death when things become unclear. The idea of death is the only thing that tempers our spirit.

Death is everywhere. It may be the headlights of a car on a hilltop in the distance behind. They may remain visible for a while, and disappear into the darkness as if they had been scooped away; only to appear on another hilltop, and then disappear again.

Those are the lights on the head of death. Death puts them on like a hat and then shoots off on a gallop, gaining on us, getting closer and closer. Sometimes it turns off its lights. But death never stops.

A warrior must know first that his acts are useless, and yet, he must proceed as if he didn't know it. That's a shaman's *controlled folly*.

The eyes of man can perform two functions: one is *seeing* energy at large as it flows in the universe and the other is "looking at things in this world." Neither of these functions is better than the other; however to train the eyes only to look is a shameful and unnecessary loss.

A warrior lives by acting, not by thinking about acting, nor by thinking about what he will think when he has finished acting.

A warrior chooses a path with heart, any path with heart, and follows it; and then he rejoices and laughs. He knows because he *sees* that his life will be over altogether too soon. He *sees* that nothing is more important than anything else.

A warrior has no honor, no dignity, no family, no name, no country; he has only life to be lived, and under these circumstances, his only tie to his fellow men is his controlled folly.

Nothing being more important than anything else, a warrior chooses any act, and acts it out as if it mattered to him. His controlled folly makes him say that what he does matters and makes him act as if it did, and yet he knows that it doesn't; so when he fulfills his acts, he retreats in peace, and whether his acts were good or bad, or worked or didn't, is in no way part of his concern.

A warrior may choose to remain totally impassive and never act, and behave as if being impassive really mattered to him; he would be rightfully true at that too, because that would also be his controlled folly.

There's no emptiness in the life of a warrior. Everything is filled to the brim. Everything is filled to the brim, and everything is equal.

An average man is too concerned with liking people or with being liked himself. A warrior likes, that's all. He likes whatever or whomever he wants, for the hell of it.

A warrior takes responsibility for his
acts, for the most trivial of his acts.
An average man acts out his thoughts,
and never takes responsibility for what
he does.

The average man is either victorious or defeated and, depending on that, he becomes a persecutor or a victim. These two conditions are prevalent as long as one does not *see*. *Seeing* dispels the illusion of victory, or defeat, or suffering.

A warrior knows that he is waiting and what he is waiting for; and while he waits he wants nothing and thus whatever little thing he gets is more than he can take. If he needs to eat he finds a way, because he is not hungry; if something hurts his body he finds a way to stop it, because he is not in pain. To be hungry or to be in pain means that the man is not a warrior; and the forces of his hunger and pain will destroy him.

Denying oneself is an indulgence. The indulgence of denying is by far the worst; it forces us to believe that we are doing great things, when in effect we are only fixed within ourselves.

Intent is not a thought, or an object, or a wish. *Intent* is what can make a man succeed when his thoughts tell him that he is defeated. It operates in spite of the warrior's indulgence. *Intent* is what makes him invulnerable. *Intent* is what sends a shaman through a wall, through space, to infinity.

When a man embarks on the warriors'
path he becomes aware, in a gradual
manner, that ordinary life has been left
forever behind. The means of the ordinary world are no longer a buffer for him;
and he must adopt a new way of life if he
is going to survive.

Every bit of knowledge that becomes power has death as its central force. Death lends the ultimate touch, and whatever is touched by death indeed becomes power.

Only the idea of death makes a warrior sufficiently detached so that he is capable of abandoning himself to anything. He knows his death is stalking him and won't give him time to cling to anything, so he tries, without craving, all of everything.

We are men and our lot is to learn and to be hurled into inconceivable new worlds. A warrior who *sees* energy knows that there is no end to the new worlds for our vision.

"Death is a twirl; death is a shiny cloud over the horizon; death is me talking to you; death is you and your writing pad; death is nothing. Nothing! It is here, yet it isn't here at all."

The spirit of a warrior is not geared to indulging and complaining, nor is it. geared to winning or losing. The spirit of a warrior is geared only to struggle, and every struggle is a warrior's last battle on earth. Thus the outcome matters very little to him. In his last battle on earth a warrior lets his spirit flow free and clear. And as he wages his battle, knowing that his *intent* is impeccable, a warrior laughs and laughs.

We talk to ourselves incessantly about our world. In fact we maintain our world with our internal talk. And whenever we finish talking to ourselves about ourselves and our world, the world is always as it should be. We renew it, we rekindle it with life, we uphold it with our internal talk. Not only that, but we also choose our paths as we talk to ourselves. Thus we repeat the same choices over and over until the day we die, because we keep on repeating the same internal talk over and over until the day we die. A warrior is aware of this and strives to stop his internal talk.

The world is all that is encased here: life, death, people, and everything else that surrounds us. The world is incomprehensible. We won't ever understand it; we won't ever unravel its secrets. Thus we must treat the world as it is: a sheer mystery.

The things that people do cannot under any conditions be more important than the world. And thus a warrior treats the world as an endless mystery and what people do as an endless folly.

Commentary

In the quotations drawn from *A Separate Reality*, the mood that the shamans of ancient Mexico affixed to all their *intentional* endeavors begins to show with remarkable clarity. Don Juan himself pointed out to me in talking about those old shamans that the aspect of their world which was of supreme interest to modern practitioners was the razor-sharp awareness that those shamans had developed about the universal force they called *intent*. They explained that the link each of those men had with such a force was so neat and clean that they could affect things to their hearts' content. Don Juan said that the *intent* of those shamans, developed to such a keen intensity, was the only aid modern practitioners had. He put it in more mundane terms, and said that modern-day practitioners, if they were honest with themselves, would pay whatever price to live under the umbrella of such an *intent*.

Don Juan asserted that anyone who showed even the slightest interest in the world of the shamans of antiquity was immediately drawn into the circle of their razor-sharp *intent*. Their *intent* was, for don Juan, something incommensurable that none of us could successfully fight away. Besides, he reasoned, there was no necessity to fight away such an *intent*, because it was the only thing that counted; it was the essence of the world of those shamans, the world which modern-day practitioners coveted more than anything imaginable.

The mood of the quotations from *A Separate Reality* is not something that I arranged on purpose. It is a mood that surfaced independent of my aims and wishes. I could even say that it was contrary to what I had in mind. It was the mysterious coil of the *wheel of time* hidden in the text of the book that had suddenly been activated, and it snapped into a state of tension: a tension that dictated the direction of my endeavors.

At the time of writing *A Separate Reality*, as far as my feelings about my work were concerned, I could truthfully assert that I thought that I was happily involved in doing anthropological fieldwork, and my feelings and thoughts were as far away from the world of the shamans of antiquity as anything could be. Don Juan had a different opinion. Being a seasoned warrior, he knew that I couldn't possibly extricate myself from the magnetic pull that the *intent* of those shamans had created. I was drowning in it, whether or not I believed in it or wished for it.

This state of affairs brought about a subliminal anxiety on my part. It was not an anxiety I could define or pinpoint, or was even aware of. It permeated my acts without the possibility of my consciously dwelling on it, or seeking an explanation. In retrospect, I can only say that I was deadly afraid, although I couldn't determine what I was afraid of.

I tried many times to analyze this sensation of fear, but I would immediately get fatigued, bored. I would instantaneously find my inquiry groundless, superfluous, and I would end up abandoning it. I asked don Juan about my state of being. I wanted his advice, his input.

"You are just afraid," he said. "That's all there is to it. Don't look for mysterious reasons for your fear. The mysterious reason is right here in front of you, within your reach. It is the *intent* of the shamans of ancient Mexico. You are dealing with their world, and that world shows its face to you from time to time. Of course, you can't take that sight. Neither could I, in my time. Neither could any one of us."

"You're talking in riddles, don Juan!"

"Yes, I am, for the moment. It will be clear to you someday. At the present, it's idiotic to try to talk about it, or explain anything. Nothing of what I'm trying to show you would make sense. Some inconceivable banality would make infinitely more sense to you at this moment."

He was absolutely right. All my fears were triggered by some banality, of which I was ashamed at the time, and am ashamed of now. I was afraid of demoniacal possession. Such a fear had been encrusted in me very early in life. Anything that was inexplicable was naturally, something evil, something malignant that aimed at destroying me.

The more poignant don Juan's explanations of the world of the ancient shamans became, the greater my sensation of needing to protect myself. This sensation was not something that could be verbalized. It was, rather than the need to protect the self, the need to protect the veracity and the undeniable value of the world in which we human beings live. To me, my world was the only recognizable world. If it was threatened, there was an immediate reaction on my part, a reaction that manifested itself in some quality of fear that I will be forever at a loss to explain; this fear was something one must feel in order to grasp its immensity. It was not the fear of dying or of being hurt. It was, rather, something immeasurably deeper than that. It was so deep that any shaman practitioner would be at a loss trying even to conceptualize it.

"You have come, in a roundabout way, to stand directly in front of the *warrior*," don Juan said.

At that time, he emphasized to no end the concept of the warrior. He said that the warrior was of course, much more than a mere concept. It was a way of life, and that way of life was the only deterrent to fear, and the only channel which a practitioner could use to let the flow of his activity move on freely. Without the concept of the warrior, the stumbling blocks on the path of knowledge were impossible to overcome.

Don Juan defined the *warrior* as the fighter par excellence. It was a mood facilitated by the *intent* of the shamans of antiquity; a mood into which any man could enter.

"The *intent* of those shamans," don Juan said, "was so keen, so powerful, that it would solidify the structure of the warrior in anyone who tapped it, even though they might not be aware of it."

In short, the warrior was, for the shamans of ancient Mexico, a unit of combat so tuned to the fight around him, so extraordinarily alert that in his purest form, he needed nothing superfluous to survive. There was no necessity to make gifts to a warrior, or to prop him up with talk or actions, or to try to give him solace and incentive. All of those things were included in the structure of the warrior itself. Since that structure was determined by the *intent* of the shamans of ancient Mexico, they made sure that anything foreseeable would be included. The end result was a fighter who fought alone and drew from his own silent convictions all the impulse he needed to forge ahead, without complaints, without the necessity to be praised.

Personally, I found the concept of the warrior fascinating, and at the same time, one of the most frightening things I had ever encountered. I thought it was a concept that, if I adopted it, would bind me into servitude, and wouldn't give me the time or the disposition to protest or examine or complain. Complaining had been my lifelong habit, and truthfully, I would have fought tooth and nail not to give it up. I thought that complaining was the sign of a sensitive, courageous, forthright man who has no qualms in stating his facts, his likes and dislikes. If all of that was going to turn into a fighting organism, I stood to lose more than I could afford.

These were my inner thoughts. And yet, I coveted the direction, the peace, the efficiency of the warrior. One of the great aids that the shamans of ancient Mexico employed in establishing the concept of the warrior was the idea of taking our death as a companion, a witness to our acts. Don Juan said that once that premise is accepted, in whatever mild form, a bridge is formed which extends across the gap between our world of daily affairs, and something that is in front of us, but has no name; something that is lost in a fog, and doesn't seem to exist; something so terribly unclear that it cannot be used as a point of reference, and yet, it is there, undeniably present.

Don Juan claimed that the only being on earth capable of crossing over that bridge was the warrior: silent in his struggle, undetainable because he has nothing to lose, functional and efficacious because he has everything to gain.

QUOTATIONS FROM
JOURNEY TO IXTLAN

We hardly ever realize that we can cut anything out of our lives, anytime, in the blink of an eye.

One shouldn't worry about taking pictures or making tape recordings. Those are superfluities of sedate lives. One should worry about the spirit, which is always receding.

A warrior doesn't need personal history. One day, he finds it is no longer necessary for him, and he drops it.

Personal history must be constantly renewed by telling parents, relatives, and friends everything one does. On the other hand, for the warrior who has no personal history, no explanations are needed; nobody is angry or disillusioned with his acts. And above all, no one pins him down with their thoughts and their expectations.

When nothing is for sure we remain alert, perennially on our toes. It is more exciting not to know which bush the rabbit is hiding behind than to behave as though we knew everything.

As long as a man feels that he is the most important thing in the world, he cannot really appreciate the world around him. He is like a horse with blinders; all he sees is himself, apart from everything else.

Death is our eternal companion. It is always to our left, an arm's length behind us. Death is the only wise adviser that a warrior has. Whenever he feels that everything is going wrong and he's about to be annihilated, he can turn to his death and ask if that is so. His death will tell him that he is wrong, that nothing really matters outside its touch. His death will tell him, 'I haven't touched you yet.'

Whenever a warrior decides to do something, he must go all the way, but he must take responsibility for what he does. No matter what he does, he must know first why he is doing it, and then he must proceed with his actions without having doubts or remorse about them.

In a world where death is the hunter, there is no time for regrets or doubts. There is only time for decisions. It doesn't matter what the decisions are. Nothing could be more or less serious than anything else. In a world where death is the hunter, there are no small or big decisions. There are only decisions that a warrior makes in the face of his inevitable death.

A warrior must learn to be available
and unavailable at the precise turn of the
road. It is useless for a warrior to be
unwittingly available at all times, as it is
useless for him to hide when everybody
knows that he is hiding.

For a warrior, to be inaccessible means that he touches the world around him sparingly. And above all, he deliberately avoids exhausting himself and others. He doesn't use and squeeze people until they have shriveled to nothing, especially the people he loves.

Once a man worries, he clings to anything out of desperation; and once he
clings he is bound to get exhausted or to
exhaust whomever or whatever he is
clinging to. A warrior-hunter, on the
other hand, knows he will lure game into
his traps over and over again, so he
doesn't worry. To worry is to become
accessible, unwittingly accessible.

A warrior-hunter deals intimately with his world, and yet he is inaccessible to that same world. He taps it lightly, stays for as long as he needs to, and then swiftly moves away, leaving hardly a mark.

To be a warrior-hunter is not just to trap game. A warrior-hunter does not catch game because he sets his traps, or because he knows the routines of his prey, but because he himself has no routines. This is his advantage. He is not at all like the animals he is after, fixed by heavy routines and predictable quirks; he is free, fluid, unpredictable.

For an average man, the world is weird because if he's not bored with it, he's at odds with it. For a warrior, the world is weird because it is stupendous, awesome, mysterious, unfathomable. A warrior must assume responsibility for being here, in this marvelous world, in this marvelous time.

A warrior must learn to make every act count, since he is going to be here in this world for only a short while, in fact, too short for witnessing all the marvels of it.

Acts have power. Especially when the warrior acting knows that those acts are his last battle. There is a strange consuming happiness in acting with the full knowledge that whatever he is doing may very well be his last act on earth.

A warrior must focus his attention on the link between himself and his death. Without remorse or sadness or worrying, he must focus his attention on the fact that he does not have time and let his acts flow accordingly. He must let each of his acts be his last battle on earth. Only under those conditions will his acts have their rightful power. Otherwise they will be, for as long as he lives, the acts of a fool.

A warrior-hunter knows that his death is waiting, and the very act he is performing now may well be his last battle on earth. He calls it a battle because it is a struggle. Most people move from act to act without any struggle or thought. A warrior-hunter, on the contrary, assesses every act; and since he has an intimate knowledge of his death, he proceeds judiciously, as if every act were his last battle. Only a fool would fail to notice the advantage a warrior-hunter has over his fellow men. A warrior-hunter gives his last battle its due respect. It's only natural that his last act on earth should be the best of himself. It's pleasurable that way. It dulls the edge of his fright.

A warrior is an immaculate hunter who hunts power; he's not drunk, or crazed, and he has neither the time nor the disposition to bluff, or to lie to himself, or to make a wrong move. The stakes are too high for that. The stakes are his trimmed orderly life which he has taken so long to tighten and perfect. He is not going to throw that away by making some stupid miscalculation, by mistaking something for something else.

A man, any man, deserves everything
that is a man's lot—joy, pain, sadness
and struggle. The nature of his acts is
unimportant as long as he acts as
a warrior.

If his spirit is distorted he should simply fix it—purge it, make it perfect—
because there is no other task in our
entire lives which is more worthwhile.
Not to fix the spirit is to seek death, and
that is the same as to seek nothing, since
death is going to overtake us regardless
of anything. To seek the perfection of the
warrior's spirit is the only task worthy of
our temporariness, and our manhood.

The hardest thing in the world is to assume the mood of a warrior. It is of no use to be sad and complain and feel justified in doing so, believing that someone is always doing something to us. Nobody is doing anything to anybody, much less to a warrior.

A warrior is a hunter. He calculates everything. That's control. Once his calculations are over, he acts. He lets go. That's abandon. A warrior is not a leaf at the mercy of the wind. No one can push him; no one can make him do things against himself or against his better judgment. A warrior is tuned to survive, and he survives in the best of all possible fashions.

A warrior is only a man, a humble man. He cannot change the designs of his death. But his impeccable spirit, which has stored power after stupendous hardships, can certainly hold his death for a moment, a moment long enough to let him rejoice for the last time in recalling his power. We may say that that is a gesture which death has with those who have an impeccable spirit.

It doesn't matter how one was brought up. What determines the way one does anything is personal power. A man is only the sum of his personal power, and that sum determines how he lives and how he dies.

100 • The Wheel of Time

Personal power is a feeling. Something like being lucky. Or one may call it a mood. Personal power is something that one acquires by means of a lifetime of struggle.

A warrior acts as if he knows what he
is doing, when in effect he knows nothing.

A warrior doesn't know remorse for anything he has done, because to isolate one's acts as being mean, or ugly, or evil is to place an unwarranted importance on the self.

The trick is in what one emphasizes. We either make ourselves miserable, or we make ourselves strong. The amount of work is the same.

People tell us from the time we are born that the world is such and such and so and so, and naturally we have no choice but to accept that the world is the way people have been telling us it is.

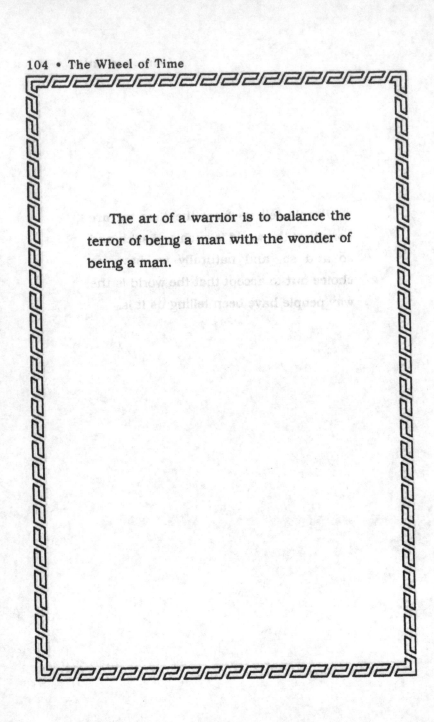

The art of a warrior is to balance the terror of being a man with the wonder of being a man.

Commentary

By the time I was writing *Journey to Ixtlan*, a most mysterious mood was prevalent all around me. Don Juan Matus was applying some extremely pragmatic measures to my daily conduct. He had outlined some steps of action that he wanted me to follow rigorously. He had given me three tasks which had only the vaguest references to my world of everyday life, or to any other world. He wanted me to endeavor in my daily world to erase my personal history by any means conceivable. Then, he wanted me to stop my routines, and finally, he wanted me to dethrone my sense of self-importance.

"How am I going to accomplish all this, don Juan?" I asked him.

"I have no idea," he responded. "None of us has any idea of how to do that pragmatically and effectively. Yet, if we start the work, we will accomplish it without ever knowing what came to aid us.

"The difficulty that you encounter is the same difficulty that I encountered myself," he went on. "I assure you that our difficulty is born out of the total absence in our lives of the idea that would spur us to change. At the time that my teacher gave me this task, all I needed in order to make it work was the idea that it could be done. Once I had the idea, I accomplished it, without knowing how. I recommend that you do the same."

I went into the most contorted complaints, alluding to the fact that I was a social scientist, accustomed to practical directions that had substance to them, not to something vague which was dependent on magical solutions rather than practical means.

"Say whatever you want," don Juan responded, laughing. "Once you're through complaining, forget about your qualms and do what I have asked you to do."

Don Juan was right. All that I needed, or rather, all that a mysterious part of me which was not overt needed, was the idea. The 'me' that I had known through all my life needed infinitely more than the idea. It needed coaching, spurring, direction. I became so intrigued by my success that the tasks of erasing my routines, losing my self-importance and dropping my personal history became a sheer delight.

"You are smack in front of the *warriors' way*," don Juan said by way of explanation for my mysterious success.

Slowly and methodically, he had guided my awareness to focus more and more intensely on an abstract elaboration of the concept of the warrior that he called the *warriors' way*, the *warriors' path*. He explained that the *warriors' way* was a structure of ideas established by the shamans of ancient Mexico. Those shamans had derived their construct by means of their ability to *see* energy as it flows freely in the universe. Therefore, the warriors' way was a most harmonious conglomerate of *energetic facts*, irreducible truths determined exclusively by the direction of the flow of energy in the universe. Don Juan categorically stated that there was nothing about the warriors' way that could be argued, nothing that could be changed. It was in itself and by itself a perfect structure, and whoever followed it was corralled by *energetic facts* that admitted no argument, no speculation about their function and their value.

Don Juan said that those old shamans called it the *warriors' way* because its structure encompassed all the living possibilities that a warrior might encounter on the path of knowledge. Those shamans were absolutely thorough and methodical in their search for such possibilities. According to don Juan, they were indeed capable of including in their abstract structure everything that is humanly possible.

Don Juan compared the warriors' way to an edifice, with each of the elements of this edifice being a propping device whose only function was to sustain the psyche of the warrior in his role of shaman initiate, in order to make his movements easy and meaningful. He stated unequivocally that the warriors' way was the essential construct without which shaman initiates would be shipwrecked in the immensity of the universe.

Don Juan called the warriors' way the crowning glory of the shamans of ancient Mexico. He viewed it as their most important contribution, the essence of their sobriety.

"Is the warriors' way that overwhelmingly important, don Juan?" I asked him once.

"'Overwhelmingly important' is a euphemism. The warriors' way is everything. It is the epitome of mental and physical health. I cannot explain it in any other way. For the shamans of ancient Mexico to have created such a structure means to me that they were at the height of their power, the peak of their happiness, the apex of their joy."

On the level of pragmatic acceptance or rejection in which I thought I was submerged at the time, to embrace the warriors' path thoroughly and unbiasedly was nothing short of an impossibility for me. The more don Juan explained the warriors' path, the more intense the sensation I had that he was indeed plotting to overthrow all my balance.

Don Juan's guidance was, therefore, covert. It manifested itself with stupendous clarity, however, in the quotations drawn from *Journey to Ixtlan*. Don Juan had advanced on me in leaps and bounds at tremendous speed, without my being aware of it, and was suddenly breathing down my neck. I thought time and time again that I was either on the verge of accepting, in a bona fide manner, the existence of another cognitive system, or I was so thoroughly indifferent that I didn't care whether it happened one way or the other.

Of course, there was always the option of running away from all that, but it wasn't tenable. Somehow, don Juan's ministrations, or my heavy use of the concept of the warrior had hardened me to the point that I was no longer that afraid. I was caught, but really, it made no difference. All I knew was that I was there with don Juan for the duration.

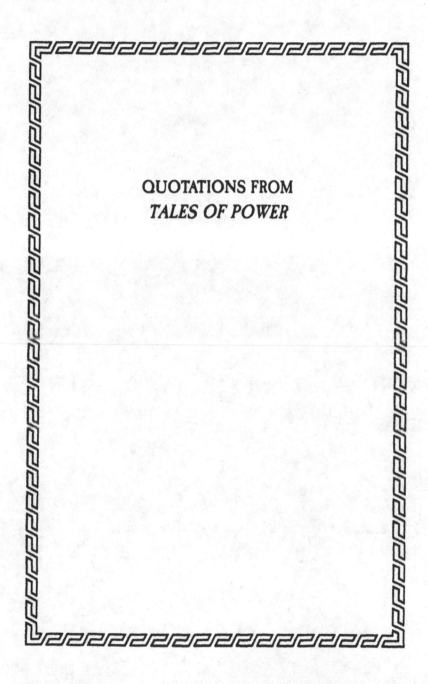

QUOTATIONS FROM
TALES OF POWER

The self-confidence of the warrior is not the self-confidence of the average man. The average man seeks certainty in the eyes of the onlooker and calls that self-confidence. The warrior seeks *impeccability* in his own eyes and calls that humbleness. The average man is hooked to his fellow men, while the warrior is hooked only to infinity.

There are lots of things a warrior can do at a certain time which he couldn't do years before. Those things themselves did not change; what changed was his idea of himself.

The only possible course that a warrior has is to act consistently and without reservations. At a certain moment, he knows enough of the warriors' way to act accordingly, but his old habits and routines may stand in his way.

> If a warrior is to succeed in anything,
> the success must come gently, with a
> great deal of effort but with no stress
> or obsession.

The *internal dialogue* is what grounds people in the daily world. The world is such and such or so and so, only because we talk to ourselves about its being such and such or so and so. The passageway into the world of shamans opens up after the warrior has learned to shut off his internal dialogue.

To change our idea of the world is the crux of shamanism. And stopping the internal dialogue is the only way to accomplish it.

When a warrior learns to stop the
internal dialogue, everything becomes
possible; the most far-fetched schemes
become attainable.

A warrior takes his lot, whatever it may be, and accepts it in ultimate humbleness. He accepts in humbleness what he is, not as grounds for regret but as a living challenge.

The humbleness of a warrior is not the humbleness of the beggar. The warrior lowers his head to no one, but at the same time, he doesn't permit anyone to lower his head to him. The beggar, on the other hand, falls to his knees at the drop of a hat and scrapes the floor for anyone he deems to be higher; but at the same time, he demands that someone lower than him scrape the floor for him.

Solace, haven, fear, all of these are words which have created moods that one has learned to accept without ever questioning their value.

Our fellow men are black magicians. And whoever is with them is a black magician on the spot. Think for a moment. Can you deviate from the path that your fellow men have lined up for you? And if you remain with them, your thoughts and your actions are fixed forever in their terms. That is slavery. The warrior, on the other hand, is free from all that. Freedom is expensive, but the price is not impossible to pay. So, fear your captors, your masters. Don't waste your time and your power fearing freedom.

The flaw with words is that they always make us feel enlightened, but when we turn around to face the world they always fail us and we end up facing the world as we always have, without enlightenment. For this reason, a warrior seeks to act rather than to talk, and to this effect, he gets a new description of the world—a new description where talking is not that important, and where new acts have new reflections.

A warrior considers himself already dead, so there is nothing for him to lose. The worst has already happened to him, therefore he's clear and calm; judging him by his acts or by his words, one would never suspect that he has witnessed everything.

Knowledge is a most peculiar affair, especially for a warrior. Knowledge for a warrior is something that comes at once, engulfs him, and passes on.

Knowledge comes to a warrior, floating, like specks of gold dust, the same dust that covers the wings of moths. So for a warrior, knowledge is like taking a shower, or being rained on by specks of dark gold dust.

Whenever the internal dialogue stops, the world collapses, and extraordinary facets of ourselves surface, as though they had been kept heavily guarded by our words.

The world is unfathomable. And so are we, and so is every being that exists in this world.

Warriors do not win victories by beating their heads against walls, but by overtaking the walls. Warriors jump over walls; they don't demolish them.

A warrior must cultivate the feeling that he has everything needed for the extravagant journey that is his life. What counts for a warrior is being alive. Life in itself is sufficient, self-explanatory and complete.

Therefore, one may say without being presumptuous that the experience of experiences is being alive.

An average man thinks that indulging in doubts and tribulations is the sign of sensitivity, spirituality. The truth of the matter is that the average man is the farthest thing imaginable from being sensitive. His puny reason deliberately makes itself into a monster or a saint, but it is truthfully too little for such a big monster or saint mold.

To be a warrior is not a simple matter of wishing to be one. It is rather an endless struggle that will go on to the very last moment of our lives. Nobody is born a warrior, in exactly the same way that nobody is born an average man. We make ourselves into one or the other.

A warrior dies the hard way. His death must struggle to take him. A warrior does not give himself to death so easily.

Human beings are not objects; they have no solidity. They are round, luminous beings; they are boundless. The world of objects and solidity is only a description that was created to help them, to make their passage on earth convenient.

Their reason makes them forget that the description is only a description, and before they realize it, human beings have entrapped the totality of themselves in a vicious circle from which they rarely emerge in their lifetimes.

Human beings are perceivers, but the world that they perceive is an illusion: an illusion created by the description that was told to them from the moment they were born.

So in essence, the world that their reason wants to sustain is the world created by a description and its dogmatic and inviolable rules, which their reason learns to accept and defend.

The concealed advantage of luminous beings is that they have something which is never used: *intent*. The maneuver of shamans is the same as the maneuver of the average man. Both have a description of the world. The average man upholds it with his reason; the shaman upholds it with his *intent*. Both descriptions have their rules; but the advantage of the shaman is that *intent* is more engulfing than reason.

Only as a warrior can one withstand the path of knowledge. A warrior cannot complain or regret anything. His life is an endless challenge, and challenges cannot possibly be good or bad. Challenges are simply challenges.

The basic difference between an ordinary man and a warrior is that a warrior takes everything as a challenge, while an ordinary man takes everything as a blessing or as a curse.

The trump card of the warrior is that he believes without believing. But obviously a warrior can't just say he believes and let it go at that. That would be too easy. To just believe without any exertion would exonerate him from examining his situation. A warrior, whenever he has to involve himself with believing, does it as a choice. A warrior doesn't believe, a warrior has to believe.

Death is the indispensable ingredient in having to believe. Without the awareness of death, everything is ordinary, trivial. It is only because death is stalking him that a warrior has to believe that the world is an unfathomable mystery. Having to believe in such a fashion is the warrior's expression of his innermost predilection.

Power always makes a cubic centimeter of chance available to a warrior. The warrior's art is to be perennially fluid in order to pluck it.

The average man is aware of everything only when he thinks he should be; the condition of a warrior, however, is to be aware of everything at all times.

The totality of ourselves is a very mysterious affair. We need only a very small portion of it to fulfill the most complex tasks of life. Yet when we die, we die with the totality of ourselves.

A rule of thumb for a warrior is that he makes his decisions so carefully that nothing that may happen as a result of them can surprise him, much less drain his power.

When a warrior makes the decision to take action, he should be prepared to die. If he is prepared to die, there shouldn't be any pitfalls, any unwelcome surprises, any unnecessary acts. Everything should gently fall into place because he is expecting nothing.

A warrior, as a teacher, must first of all teach about the possibility of acting without believing, without expecting rewards—acting just for the hell of it. His success as a teacher depends on how well and how harmoniously he guides his wards in this specific respect.

In order to help his ward to erase personal history, the warrior as a teacher teaches three techniques: losing self-importance, assuming responsibility for one's acts, and using death as an adviser. Without the beneficial effect of these three techniques, erasing personal history would involve being shifty, evasive and unnecessarily dubious about oneself and one's actions.

There is no way to get rid of self-pity
for good; it has a definite place and
character in our lives, a definite facade
which is recognizable. Thus, every time
the occasion arises, the facade of self-pity
becomes active. It has a history. But
if one changes the facade, one shifts its
place of prominence.

One changes facades by shifting the
component elements of the facade itself.
Self-pity is useful to the user because he
feels important and deserving of better
conditions, better treatment, or because
he is unwilling to assume responsibility
for the acts that brought him to the state
that elicited self-pity.

Changing the facade of self-pity means only that one has assigned a secondary place to a formerly important element. Self-pity is still a prominent feature; but it has now taken a position in the background, in the same fashion that the idea of one's impending death, the idea of a warrior's humbleness, or the idea of responsibility for one's acts were all in the background at one time for a warrior, without ever being used until the moment he became a warrior.

A warrior acknowledges his pain but he doesn't indulge in it. The mood of the warrior who enters into the unknown is not one of sadness; on the contrary, he's joyful because he feels humbled by his great fortune, confident that his spirit is impeccable, and above all, fully aware of his efficiency. A warrior's joyfulness comes from having accepted his fate, and from having truthfully assessed what lies ahead of him.

Commentary

Tales of Power is the mark of my ultimate downfall. At the time that the events narrated in that book took place, I suffered a profound emotional upheaval, a warrior's breakdown. Don Juan Matus left this world, and left his four apprentices in it. Each of those apprentices was approached personally by don Juan, and assigned a specific task. I considered the task given to me to be a placebo that had no significance whatsoever in comparison to the loss.

Not to see don Juan anymore could not be soothed by pseudo-tasks. My first plea with don Juan was, naturally, to tell him that I wanted to go with him.

"You are not ready, yet," he said. "Let's be realistic."

"But I could make myself ready in the blink of an eye," I assured him.

"I don't doubt that. You'll be ready, but not for me. I demand perfect efficiency. I demand an impeccable *intent*, an impeccable discipline. You don't have that yet. You will, you're coming to it, but you're not there yet.

"You have the power to take me, don Juan. Raw and imperfect."

"I suppose I do, but I won't, because it would be a shameful waste for you. You stand to lose everything, take my word. Don't insist. Insisting is not in the realm of warriors."

That statement was sufficient to stop me. Internally, however, I yearned to go with him, to venture beyond the boundaries of everything that I knew as normal and real.

When the moment came in which don Juan actually left the world, he turned into some colored, vaporous luminosity. He was pure energy, flowing freely in the universe. My sensation of loss was so immense at that moment that I wanted to die. I disregarded everything don Juan had said, and without any hesitation, I proceeded to throw myself off a precipice. I reasoned that if I did that, in death, don Juan would have been obliged to take me with him, and save whatever bit of awareness was left in me.

But for reasons that are inexplicable, whether I view it from the premises of my normal cognition, or from the cognition of the shamans' world, I didn't die. I was left alone in the world of everyday life, while my three cohorts were scattered all over the world. I was unknown to myself, something which made my loneliness more poignant than ever.

I saw myself as an agent provocateur, a spy of sorts, that don Juan had left behind for some obscure reasons. The quotations drawn from the corpus of *Tales of Power* show the unknown quality of the world, not the world of shamans, but the world of everyday life, which, according to don Juan, is as mysterious and rich as anything can be. All we need to pluck the wonders of this world of everyday life is enough detachment. But more than detachment, we need enough affection and abandon.

"A warrior must love this world," don Juan had warned me, "in order for this world that seems so commonplace to open up and show its wonders."

We were, at the time that he voiced this statement, in the desert of Sonora.

"It is a sublime feeling," he said, "to be in this marvelous desert, to see those ragged peaks of pseudo-mountains that were really made by the flow of lava of long-gone volcanoes. It is a glorious feeling to find that some of those nuggets of obsidian were created at such high temperatures that they still retain the mark of their origin. They have power galore. To wander aimlessly in those ragged peaks and actually find a piece of quartz that picks up radio waves is extraordinary. The only drawback to this marvelous picture is that to enter into the marvels of this world, or into the marvels of another world, a man needs to be a warrior: calm, collected, indifferent, seasoned by the onslaughts of the unknown. You are not seasoned that way yet. Therefore, it is your duty to seek that fulfillment before you could talk about venturing into the infinite."

I have spent thirty-five years of my life seeking the maturity of a warrior. I have gone to places that defy description, seeking that sensation of being seasoned by the onslaughts of the unknown. I went unobtrusively, unannounced, and I came back in the same fashion. The works of warriors are silent and solitary, and when warriors go, or come back, they do it so inconspicuously that nobody is the wiser. To seek a warrior's maturity in any other fashion would be ostentatious, and therefore, inadmissible.

The quotations from *Tales of Power* were the most poignant reminder to me that the *intent* of the shamans who lived in Mexico in ancient times was still impeccably at work. The *wheel of time* was moving inexorably around me, forcing me to look into grooves which one cannot talk about and still remain coherent.

"Suffice it to say," don Juan said to me once, "that the immensity of this world, be it the shamans' world or the average man's, is so conspicuous that only an aberration could keep us from noticing it. Trying to explain to aberrant beings what it is like to be lost in the grooves of the *wheel of time* is the most absurd thing that a warrior can undertake. Therefore, he makes sure that his journeys are only the property of his condition of being a warrior."

QUOTATIONS FROM
THE SECOND RING OF POWER

When one has nothing to lose, one becomes courageous. We are timid only when there is something we can still cling to.

A warrior could not possibly leave anything to chance. He actually affects the outcome of events by the force of his awareness and his *unbending intent*.

If a warrior wants to pay back for all the favors he has received, and he has no one in particular to address his payment to, he can address it to the spirit of man. That's always a very small account, and whatever one puts in it is more than enough.

After arranging the world in a most beautiful and enlightened manner, the scholar goes back home at five o'clock in the afternoon in order to forget his beautiful arrangement.

The *human form* is a conglomerate of energy fields which exists in the universe, and which is related exclusively to human beings. Shamans call it the *human form* because those energy fields have been bent and contorted by a lifetime of habits and misuse.

A warrior knows that he cannot change, and yet he makes it his business to try to change, nevertheless. The warrior is never disappointed when he fails to change. That's the only advantage a warrior has over the average man.

Warriors must be impeccable in their effort to change, in order to scare the human form and shake it away. After years of impeccability, a moment will come when the human form cannot stand it any longer and leaves. That is to say, a moment will come when the energy fields contorted by a lifetime of habit are straightened out. A warrior gets deeply affected, and can even die as a result of this straightening out of energy fields, but an impeccable warrior always survives.

The only freedom warriors have is to behave impeccably. Not only is impeccability freedom; it is the only way to straighten out the human form.

Any habit needs all its parts in order
to function. If some parts are missing,
the habit is disassembled.

The fight is right here on this earth.
We are human creatures. Who knows
what's waiting for us, or what kind of
power we may have?

The world of people goes up and down and people go up and down with their world; warriors have no business following the ups and downs of their fellow men.

The core of our being is the act of perceiving, and the magic of our being is the act of awareness. Perception and awareness are a single, functional, inextricable unit.

We choose only once. We choose either to be warriors or to be ordinary men. A second choice does not exist. Not on this earth.

The warriors' way offers a man a new life and that life has to be completely new. He can't bring to that new life his ugly old ways.

Warriors always take a first event of any series as the blueprint or the map of what is going to develop for them subsequently.

Human beings love to be told what to do, but they love even more to fight and not do what they are told, and thus they get entangled in hating the one who told them in the first place.

Everybody has enough personal power for something. The trick for the warrior is to pull his personal power away from his weaknesses to his warrior's purpose.

Everyone can *see*, and yet we choose
not to remember what we *see*.

Commentary

Years went by before I wrote *The Second Ring of Power*. Don Juan was long gone, and the quotations from that book are memories of what he had said, memories triggered by a new situation, a new development. Another player had appeared in my life. It was don Juan's cohort, Florinda Matus. All of don Juan's apprentices understood that when don Juan left, Florinda was left behind to somehow round up the last part of our training.

"Not until you are capable of taking orders from a woman without detriment to your being will you be complete," don Juan had said. "But that woman cannot be any woman. It must be somebody special, somebody who has power, and a quality of ruthlessness that will not allow you to be the man-in-charge that you fancy yourself to be."

Of course, I laughed off his statements. I thought he was definitely joking. The truth of the matter was that he wasn't joking at all. One day, Florinda Donner-Grau and Taisha Abelar returned, and we went to Mexico. We went to a department store in the city of Guadalajara, and there, we found Florinda Matus, the most gorgeous woman I had ever seen: extremely tall—five feet eleven, lean, angular, with a beautiful face, old, and yet very young.

"Ah! There you are!" she exclaimed, when she saw us. "The Three Musketeers! The Pep Boys—Eenie, Meenie and Mo! I've been looking for you all over!"

And without any more to say, she took over. Florinda Donner-Grau, of course, was delighted beyond measure. Taisha Abelar was extremely reserved, as usual, and I was mortified, almost furious. I knew that the arrangement was not going to work. I was ready to clash with this woman the first time she opened her daring mouth and came up with shit like "Eenie, Meenie and Mo—the Pep Boys."

Unsuspected things that I had in reserve, however, came to my aid, and prevented me from any reaction of wrath or annoyance, and I got along with Florinda superbly, better than I could have dreamed. She ruled us with an iron hand. She was the undisputed queen of our lives. She had the power, the detachment, to carry out her job of tuning us in the most subtle way. She didn't allow us to drown in self-pity or complaining if something was not quite to our liking. She was not at all like don Juan. She lacked his sobriety, but she had another quality that balanced her lack: she was as fast as anything could be. One glance was sufficient for her to comprehend an entire situation, and to act instantaneously in accordance with what was expected of her.

One of her favorite ploys, which I enjoyed immensely, was to formally ask an audience, or a group of people she was talking to, "Does anyone here know anything about the pressure and displacement of gases?" She would ask such a question in true seriousness. And when the audience responded, "No, no, we don't," she would say, "Then, I could say anything I want, true?!"—and indeed she would go ahead and say anything she wanted. She would actually sometimes say such ridiculous things that I would fall on the floor laughing.

Her other classical question was, "Does anyone here know anything about the retina of chimpanzees? No?"—and Florinda would say barbarities about the retina of chimpanzees. Never in my life had I enjoyed my time more thoroughly. I was her admirer and unbiased follower.

I once had a fistula by the crest of the bone of my hip, a product of a fall that I had taken years before into a ravine filled with cactus needles. There had been seventy-five needles stuck in my body. One of them either hadn't come out completely or had left a residue of dirt or debris that years later produced a fistula.

My doctor said, "That's nothing. It is just a sack of pus that has to be lanced. It's a very simple operation. It would take a few minutes to clean it out."

I consulted with Florinda, and she said, "You are the nagual. You either cure yourself, or you die. No shades of meaning, no double behavior. For a nagual to be lanced by a doctor—you must have lost your power. For a nagual to die fistulated? What a shame."

Except for Florinda Donner-Grau and Taisha Abelar, the rest of don Juan's apprentices didn't care at all for Florinda. She was a threatening figure. She was someone who never allowed them the freedom that they felt was their due. She never celebrated their pseudo-exploits of shamanism, and she stopped their activities every time they strayed from the warriors' path.

In the corpus of *The Second Ring of Power*, that struggle of the apprentices is more than manifest. Don Juan's other apprentices were a lost lot, filled with egomaniacal outbursts, each one pulling in his own direction, each one asserting his or her value.

Everything that took place in our lives from that time on was deeply influenced by Florinda Matus, and yet, she never took the front stand. She was always a figure in the background, wise, funny, ruthless. Florinda Donner-Grau and I learned to love her as we had never loved before, and when she left, she willed to Florinda Donner-Grau her name, her jewels, her money, her grace, her savoir-faire. I felt that I could never write a book about Florinda Matus, that if anybody ever did, it would have to be Florinda Donner-Grau, her true heir, her daughter of daughters. I was, like Florinda Matus, only a figure in the background, put there by don Juan Matus to break the loneliness of a warrior, and enjoy my passage on earth.

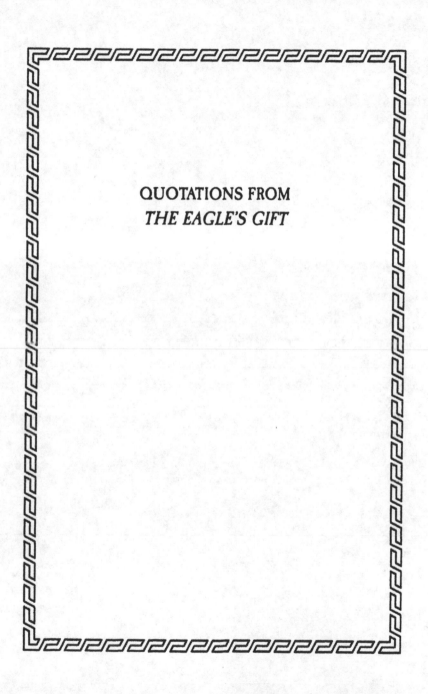

QUOTATIONS FROM
THE EAGLE'S GIFT

The art of *dreaming* is the capacity to utilize one's ordinary dreams and transform them into controlled awareness by virtue of a specialized form of attention called the *dreaming attention*.

The art of *stalking* is a set of procedures and attitudes that enables a warrior to get the best out of any conceivable situation.

The recommendation for warriors is not to have any material things on which to focus their power, but to focus it on the spirit, on the true flight into the unknown, not on trivialities.

Everyone who wants to follow the warrior's path has to rid himself of the compulsion to possess and hold onto things.

Seeing is a bodily knowledge. The predominance of the visual sense in us influences this bodily knowledge and makes it seem to be eye-related.

Losing the human form is like a spiral. It gives a warrior the freedom to remember himself as straight fields of energy and this in turn makes him even freer.

A warrior knows that he is waiting, and he knows what he is waiting for, and while he waits, he feasts his eyes upon the world. A warrior's ultimate accomplishment is to enjoy the joy of infinity.

The course of a warrior's destiny is unalterable. The challenge is how far he can go and how impeccable he can be within those rigid bounds.

People's actions no longer affect a warrior when he has no more expectations of any kind. A strange peace becomes the ruling force in his life. He has adopted one of the concepts of a warrior's life—detachment.

Detachment does not automatically mean wisdom, but it is, nonetheless, an advantage because it allows the warrior to pause momentarily to reassess situations, to reconsider positions. In order to use that extra moment consistently and correctly, however, a warrior has to struggle unyieldingly for the duration of his life.

I am already given to the power that
rules my fate.
And I cling to nothing, so I will have
nothing to defend.
I have no thoughts, so I will see.
I fear nothing, so I will remember myself.

Detached and at ease,
I will dart past the Eagle to be free.

It is much easier for warriors to fare well under conditions of maximum stress than to be impeccable under normal circumstances.

Human beings are two-sided. The right side encompasses everything the intellect can conceive of. The left side is a realm of indescribable features; a realm impossible to contain in words. The left side is perhaps comprehended, if comprehension is what takes place, with the total body; thus its resistance to conceptualization.

All the faculties, possibilities, and accomplishments of shamanism, from the simplest to the most astounding, are in the human body itself.

The power that governs the destiny of all living beings is called the *Eagle*, not because it is an eagle or has anything to do with an eagle, but because it appears to the eye of the seer as an immeasurable jet-black eagle, standing erect as an eagle stands, its height reaching to infinity.

The Eagle devours the awareness of all the creatures that, alive on earth a moment before and now dead, have floated to the Eagle's beak like a swarm of fireflies, to meet their owner, their reason for having had life. The Eagle disentangles these tiny flames, lays them flat, as a tanner stretches out a hide, and then consumes them; for awareness is the Eagle's food.

The Eagle, that power that governs
the destinies of all living things, reflects
equally and at once all those living
things. There is no way, therefore, for
man to pray to the Eagle, to ask favors,
to hope for grace. The human part of
the Eagle is too insignificant to move
the whole.

Every living thing has been granted the power, if it so desires, to seek an opening to freedom and go through it. It is evident to the seer who *sees* the opening, and to the creatures that go through it, that the Eagle has granted that gift in order to perpetuate awareness.

To cross over to freedom does not
mean eternal life as eternity is common-
ly understood—that is, as living forever.
Rather, warriors can keep their awareness, which is ordinarily relinquished at
the moment of dying. At the moment of
crossing, the body in its entirety is kindled with knowledge. Every cell at once
becomes aware of itself and also aware of
the totality of the body.

The Eagle's gift of freedom is not a
bestowal, but a chance to have a chance.

A warrior is never under siege. To be under siege implies that one has personal possessions that could be blockaded. A warrior has nothing in the world except his impeccability, and impeccability cannot be threatened.

The first principle of the art of stalking
is that warriors choose their battleground.
A warrior never goes into battle without
knowing what the surroundings are.

To discard everything that is unnecessary is the second principle of the art of
stalking. A warrior doesn't complicate
things. He aims at being simple. He
applies all the concentration he has to
decide whether or not to enter into battle,
for any battle is a battle for his life. This
is the third principle of the art of stalking. A warrior must be willing and ready
to make his last stand here and now. But
not in a helter-skelter way.

A warrior relaxes and abandons himself; he fears nothing. Only then will the powers that guide human beings open the road for a warrior and aid him. Only then. That is the fourth principle of the art of stalking.

When faced with odds that cannot be dealt with, warriors retreat for a moment. They let their minds meander. They occupy their time with something else. Anything would do. That is the fifth principle of the art of stalking.

Warriors compress time; this is the sixth principle of the art of stalking. Even an instant counts. In a battle for your life, a second is an eternity, an eternity that may decide the outcome. Warriors aim at succeeding, therefore they compress time. Warriors don't waste an instant.

In order to apply the seventh principle of the art of stalking, one has to apply the other six: a stalker never pushes himself to the front. He is always looking on from behind the scenes.

Applying these principles brings about three results. The first is that stalkers learn never to take themselves seriously; they learn to laugh at themselves. If they are not afraid of being a fool, they can fool anyone. The second is that stalkers learn to have endless patience. Stalkers are never in a hurry; they never fret. And the third is that stalkers learn to have an endless capacity to improvise.

Warriors face the oncoming time. Normally we face time as it recedes from us. Only warriors can change that and face time as it advances on them.

Warriors have only one thing in mind: their freedom. To die and be eaten by the Eagle is no challenge. On the other hand, to sneak around the Eagle and be free is the ultimate audacity.

When warriors talk about time, they are not referring to something which is measured by the movement of a clock. Time is the essence of attention; the Eagle's emanations are made out of time; and properly speaking, when a warrior enters into other aspects of the self, he is becoming acquainted with time.

A warrior can no longer weep, and his only expression of anguish is a shiver that comes from the very depths of the universe. It is as if one of the Eagle's emanations were made out of pure anguish, and when it hits a warrior, the warrior's shiver is infinite.

Commentary

It was a remarkable sensation for me to examine the quotations drawn from *The Eagle's Gift*. I felt immediately the hard coil of the *intent* of the shamans of ancient Mexico working as vividly as ever. I knew then, beyond the shadow of a doubt, that the quotations from this book were ruled by their *wheel of time*. Further, I knew that this had been the case with everything I had done in the past, such as writing *The Eagle's Gift*, and that it is the case with everything I do, as in writing the present book.

Since I am at a loss to elucidate this matter, the only option open to me is to accept it in humbleness. The shamans of ancient Mexico did have another cognitive system at work, and from the units of that cognitive system, they could still affect me today in the most positive, uplifting fashion.

Due to the effort of Florinda Matus, who engaged me in learning the most elaborate variations of standard shamanistic techniques devised by the shamans of ancient times, such as the recapitulation, I was able to view, for instance, my experiences with don Juan with a force I never could have imagined. The corpus of my book, *The Eagle's Gift*, is the result of such views that I had of don Juan Matus.

For don Juan Matus, to recapitulate meant to relive and rearrange everything of one's life in one single sweep. He never bothered with the minutiae of elaborate variations of that ancient technique. Florinda, on the other hand, had an entirely different meticulousness. She spent months coaching me to enter into aspects of recapitulating that I am to this day at a loss to explain.

"It is the vastness of the warrior which you are experiencing," she explained. "The techniques are there. Big deal. What is of supreme importance is the man using them, and his desire to go all the way with them."

To recapitulate don Juan in Florinda's terms resulted in views of don Juan of the most excruciating detail and meaning. It was infinitely more intense than talking to don Juan himself. It was Florinda's pragmatism that gave me astounding insights into practical possibilities that were not in the least the concern of the nagual Juan Matus. Florinda, being a true woman pragmatist, had no illusions about herself, no dreams of grandeur. She said that she was a plower who could not afford to miss a single turn of the way.

"A warrior must go very slowly," she recommended, "and make use of every available item on the warriors' path. One of the most remarkable items is the capacity we all have, as warriors, to focus our attention with unwavering force on events lived. Warriors can even focus it on people they have never met. The end result of this deep focusing is always the same. It reconstructs the scene. Whole chunks of behavior, forgotten or brand new, make themselves available to a warrior. Try it."

I followed her advice, and of course, I focused on don Juan, and I remembered everything that had transpired at any given moment. I remembered details that I had no business remembering. Thanks to the work of Florinda, I was able to reconstruct enormous chunks of activity with don Juan, as well as details of tremendous importance that had bypassed me completely.

The spirit of the quotations from *The Eagle's Gift* was most shocking to me because the quotations revealed the profound emphasis that don Juan had put on the items of his world, on the warriors' way as the epitome of human accomplishment. That drive had survived his person, and was as alive as ever. Sometimes, I sincerely felt that don Juan had never left. I got to the point of actually hearing him moving around the house. I asked Florinda about it.

She said, "Oh, that's nothing. It's just the nagual Juan Matus's emptiness that reaches out to touch you, no matter where his awareness is at the moment."

Her answer left me more puzzled, more intrigued, and more despondent than ever. Although Florinda was the closest person to the nagual Juan Matus, they were astoundingly different. One thing that they both shared was the emptiness of their persons. They were no longer people. Don Juan Matus did not exist as a person. But what existed instead of his person was a collection of stories, each of them apropos to the situation he was discussing, didactic stories and jokes that bore the mark of his sobriety and his frugality.

Florinda was the same; she had stories upon stories. But her stories were about people. They were like a high form of gossip, or gossip elevated, due to her impersonality, to inconceivable heights of effectiveness and enjoyment.

"I want you to examine one man who bears a tremendous resemblance to you," she said one day to me. "I want you to recapitulate him as if you had known him all your life. This man was transcendental in the formation of our lineage. His name was Elias, the nagual Elias. I call him 'the nagual who lost heaven.'

"The story is that the nagual Elias was reared by a Jesuit priest, who taught him to read and write and to play the harpsichord. He taught him Latin. The nagual Elias could read the scriptures in Latin as fluently as any scholar could. His destiny was to be a priest, but he was an Indian, and Indians in those days did not fit into clerical hierarchies. They were too awe-some-looking, too dark, too Indian. Priests were from the upper social classes, descendants of Spaniards, with white skin, blue eyes; they were handsome, presentable. The nagual Elias was a bear in comparison, but he struggled long, kindled by his mentor's promise that God would see that he was accepted into the priesthood.

"He was the sexton of the church where his mentor was the parish priest, and one day, an actual witch walked in. Her name was Amalia. They say that she was a wild card. Be that as it may, she ended up seducing the poor sexton, who fell so deeply, so hopelessly in love with Amalia that he ended up in the hut of a nagual man. In time, he became the nagual Elias, a figure to reckon with, cultured, well-read. It seemed that the niche of nagual was made for him. It allowed him the anonymity and the effectiveness that was denied him in the world.

"He was a dreamer, and so good at it that he covered the most recondite places of the universe in a bodiless state. Sometimes he even brought back objects that had attracted his eye because of the lines of their design, objects that were incomprehensible. He called them 'inventions.' He had a whole collection of them.

"I want you to focus your recapitulation attention on those inventions," Florinda commanded me. "I want you to end up sniffing them, feeling them with your hands, although you have never seen them except through what I am telling you now. To do this focusing means to establish a point of reference, as in an algebraic equation in which something is calculated by playing on a third element. You'll be able to see the nagual Juan Matus with infinite clarity, using someone else as a point of corroboration."

The corpus of the book *The Eagle's Gift* is a review in depth of what don Juan had done to me while he was in the world. The views that I had of don Juan due to my new recapitulation skills—using the nagual Elias as a point of corroboration—were infinitely more intense than any views that I had of him while he was alive.

The recapitulation views I was engaged in lacked the warmth of the living, but they had instead the precision and the accuracy of inanimate objects that one can examine to one's heart's content.

QUOTATIONS FROM
THE FIRE FROM WITHIN

There is no completeness without sadness and longing, for without them there is no sobriety, no kindness. Wisdom without kindness and knowledge without sobriety are useless.

Self-importance is man's greatest enemy. What weakens him is feeling offended by the deeds and misdeeds of his fellow men. Self-importance requires that one spend most of one's life offended by something or someone.

In order to follow the path of knowledge,
one has to be very imaginative. On the path
of knowledge, nothing is as clear as we'd
like it to be.

If seers can hold their own in facing petty tyrants, they can certainly face the unknown with impunity, and then they can even withstand the presence of the unknowable.

What seems natural is to think that
a warrior who can hold his own in the
face of the unknown can certainly face
petty tyrants with impunity. But that's
not necessarily so. What destroyed the
superb warriors of ancient times was to
rely on that assumption. Nothing can
temper the spirit of a warrior as much as
the challenge of dealing with impossible
people in positions of power. Only under
those conditions can warriors acquire the
sobriety and serenity to withstand the
pressure of the unknowable.

The unknown is something that is veiled from man, shrouded perhaps by a terrifying context, but which, nonetheless, is within man's reach. The unknown becomes the known at a given time. The unknowable, on the other hand, is the indescribable, the unthinkable, the unrealizable. It is something that will never be known to us, and yet it is there, dazzling and at the same time horrifying in its vastness.

We perceive. This is a hard fact. But
what we perceive is not a fact of the same
kind, because we learn what to perceive.

Warriors say that we think there is a world of objects out there only because of our awareness. But what's really out there are the Eagle's emanations, fluid, forever in motion, and yet unchanged, eternal.

The deepest flaw of unseasoned warriors is that they are willing to forget the wonder of what they *see*. They become overwhelmed by the fact that they *see* and believe that it's their genius that counts. A seasoned warrior must be a paragon of discipline in order to override the nearly invincible laxness of our human condition. More important than *seeing* itself is what warriors do with what they *see*.

One of the greatest forces in the lives
of warriors is fear, because it spurs them
to learn.

For a seer, the truth is that all living beings are struggling to die. What stops death is awareness.

The unknown is forever present, but it is outside the possibility of our normal awareness. The unknown is the superfluous part of the average man. And it is superfluous because the average man doesn't have enough free energy to grasp it.

The greatest flaw of human beings is to remain glued to the inventory of reason. Reason doesn't deal with man as energy. Reason deals with instruments that create energy, but it has never seriously occurred to reason that we are better than instruments: we are organisms that create energy. We are bubbles of energy.

Warriors who deliberately attain total awareness are a sight to behold. That is the moment when they burn from within. The fire from within consumes them. And in full awareness they fuse themselves to the emanations of the Eagle at large, and glide into eternity.

Once *inner silence* is attained, everything is possible. The way to stop talking to ourselves is to use exactly the same method used to teach us to talk to ourselves; we were taught compulsively and unwaveringly, and this is the way we must stop it: compulsively and unwaveringly.

Impeccability begins with a single act that has to be deliberate, precise, and sustained. If that act is repeated long enough, one acquires a sense of unbending *intent*, which can be applied to anything else. If that is accomplished the road is clear. One thing will lead to another until the warrior realizes his full potential.

The mystery of awareness is darkness. Human beings reek of that mystery, of things which are inexplicable. To regard ourselves in any other terms is madness. So a warrior doesn't demean the mystery of man by trying to rationalize it.

Realizations are of two kinds. One is just pep talk, great outbursts of emotion and nothing more. The other is the product of a shift of the assemblage point; it is not coupled with an emotional outburst, but with action. The emotional realizations come years later after warriors have solidified, by usage, the new position of their assemblage points.

The worst that could happen to us is that we have to die, and since that is already our unalterable fate, we are free; those who have lost everything no longer have anything to fear.

Warriors don't venture into the unknown out of greed. Greed works only in the world of ordinary affairs. To venture into that terrifying loneliness of the unknown, one must have something greater than greed: love. One needs love for life, for intrigue, for mystery. One needs unquenchable curiosity and guts galore.

A warrior thinks only of the mysteries of awareness; mystery is all that matters. We are living beings; we have to die and relinquish our awareness. But if we could change just a tinge of that, what mysteries must await us? What mysteries!

Commentary

The Fire from Within as a book was another of the end results of the influence of Florinda Matus on my life. She guided me to focus this time on don Juan's teacher, the nagual Julian. Both Florinda and my detailed focusing on the man revealed to me that the nagual Julian Osorio had been an actor of some merit—but more than an actor, he had been a licentious man, concerned exclusively with the seduction of women, women of any kind with whom he came in contact during his theatrical presentations. He was so extremely licentious that ultimately, his health failed, and he became infected with tuberculosis.

His teacher, the nagual Elias, found him one afternoon in an open field on the outskirts of the city of Durango, seducing the daughter of a wealthy landowner. Due to the exertion, the actor began to hemorrhage, and the hemorrhage became so heavy that he was on the brink of dying. Florinda said that the nagual Elias *saw* that there was no way for him to help him. To cure the actor was an impossibility, and the only thing that he could do as a nagual was to arrest the bleeding, which he did. He saw fit to make then a proposition to the actor.

"I'm leaving at five in the morning for the mountains," he said. "Be at the entrance of the town. Don't fail. If you fail to come, you will die, sooner than you think. Your only recourse is to go with me. I'll never be able to cure you, but I will be able to deviate your inexorable walk to the abyss that marks the end of life. All of us human beings go inexorably into that abyss sooner or later. I will head you off to walk the enormous extent of that crack, either to the left or to the right of it. As long as you don't fall, you will live. You'll never be well, but you'll live."

The nagual Elias didn't have great expectations about the actor, who was lazy, slovenly, self-indulgent, perhaps even a coward. He was quite surprised when the next day at five in the morning he found the actor waiting for him at the edge of the town. He took him to the mountains, and in time, the actor became the nagual Julian—a tubercular man who was never cured, but who lived to be perhaps one hundred and seven years old, always walking along the edge of the abyss.

"Of course, it is of supreme importance to you," Florinda said to me once, "that you examine the walk of the nagual Julian along the edge of the abyss. The nagual Juan Matus didn't care to know anything about it. To him, all of that was superfluous. You're not as talented as the nagual Juan Matus. Nothing can be superfluous for you, as a warrior. You must allow the thoughts, the feelings, the ideas of the shamans of ancient Mexico to come to you freely."

Florinda was right. I don't have the splendor of the nagual Juan Matus. Just as she had said, nothing could be superfluous to me. I needed every prop, every twist. I could not afford to bypass any of the views or ideas of the shamans of ancient Mexico, no matter how far-fetched they might have seemed to me.

To examine the walk of the nagual Julian on the edge of the abyss meant that the ability to focus my recollection could be extended to the feelings that the nagual Julian had about his most extraordinary struggle to remain alive. I was shocked to the marrow of my bones to find out that the struggle of that man was a second-to-second fight, with his terrifying habits of indulging and his extraordinary sensuality pitted against his rigid adherence to survival. His fight was not sporadic; it was a most sustained, disciplined struggle to remain balanced. Walking on the edge of the abyss meant the battle of a warrior enhanced to such a degree that every second counted. One single moment of weakness would have thrown the nagual Julian into that abyss.

However, if he kept his view, his emphasis, his concern focused on what Florinda called the edge of the abyss, the pressure eased. Whatever he was viewing was not as desperate as what he was viewing when his old habits began to take hold of him. It seemed to me that when I looked at the nagual Julian at those moments, I was recapitulating a different man; a man more peaceful, more detached, more collected.

QUOTATIONS FROM
THE POWER OF SILENCE

It isn't that a warrior learns shamanism as time goes by; rather, what he
learns as time goes by is to save energy.
This energy will enable him to handle
some of the energy fields which are ordinarily inaccessible to him. Shamanism is
a state of awareness, the ability to use
energy fields that are not employed in
perceiving the everyday-life world that
we know.

In the universe there is an immeasurable, indescribable force which shamans call *intent*, and absolutely everything that exists in the entire cosmos is attached to *intent* by a connecting link. Warriors are concerned with discussing, understanding, and employing that connecting link. They are especially concerned with cleaning it of the numbing effects brought about by the ordinary concerns of their everyday lives. Shamanism at this level can be defined as the procedure of cleaning one's connecting link to *intent*.

Shamans are vitally concerned with their past, but not their personal past. For shamans, their past is what other shamans in bygone days have accomplished. They consult their past in order to obtain a point of reference. Only shamans genuinely seek a point of reference in their past. For them, establishing a point of reference means a chance to examine *intent*.

The average man also examines the past. But it's his personal past he examines, for personal reasons. He measures himself against the past, whether his personal past or the past knowledge of his time, in order to find justifications for his present or future behavior, or to establish a model for himself.

The spirit manifests itself to a warrior at every turn. However, this is not the entire truth. The entire truth is that the spirit reveals itself to everyone with the same intensity and consistency, but only warriors are consistently attuned to such revelations.

Warriors speak of shamanism as a magical, mysterious bird which has paused in its flight for a moment in order to give man hope and purpose; warriors live under the wing of that bird, which they call the *bird of wisdom*, the *bird of freedom*.

For a warrior, the spirit is an abstract only because he knows it without words or even thoughts. It's an abstract because he can't conceive what the spirit is. Yet, without the slightest chance or desire to understand it, a warrior handles the spirit. He recognizes it, beckons it, entices it, becomes familiar with it, and expresses it with his acts.

The average man's connecting link with *intent* is practically dead, and warriors begin with a link that is useless, because it does not respond voluntarily. In order to revive that link, warriors need a rigorous, fierce purpose—a special state of mind called *unbending intent.*

The power of man is incalculable; death exists only because we have *intended* it since the moment of our birth. The *intent* of death can be suspended by making the assemblage point change positions.

The art of stalking is learning all the quirks of your disguise, and learning them so well that no one will know you are disguised. For that you need to be ruthless, cunning, patient and sweet. Ruthlessness should not be harshness, cunning should not be cruelty, patience should not be negligence, and sweetness should not be foolishness.

Warriors have an ulterior purpose for their acts, which has nothing to do with personal gain. The average man acts only if there is the chance for profit. Warriors act not for profit, but for the spirit.

The shaman seers of ancient times, through their *seeing*, first noticed that any unusual behavior produced a tremor in the assemblage point. They soon discovered that if unusual behavior is practiced systematically and directed wisely, it eventually forces the assemblage point to move.

Silent knowledge is nothing but direct
contact with *intent*.

Shamanism is a journey of return. A warrior returns victorious to the spirit, having descended into hell. And from hell he brings trophies. Understanding is one of his trophies.

Warriors, because they are stalkers, understand human behavior to perfection. They understand, for instance, that human beings are creatures of inventory. Knowing the ins and outs of a particular inventory is what makes a man a scholar or an expert in his field.

Warriors know that when an average person's inventory fails, the person either enlarges his inventory or his world of self-reflection collapses. The average person is able to incorporate new items into his inventory if the new items don't contradict the inventory's underlying order. But if the items contradict that order, the person's mind collapses. The inventory is the mind. Warriors count on this when they attempt to break the mirror of self-reflection.

Warriors can never make a bridge to join the people of the world. But, if people desire to do so, they have to make a bridge to join warriors.

In order for the mysteries of shamanism to be available to anyone, the spirit
must descend onto whoever is interested.
The spirit lets its presence by itself move
the man's assemblage point to a specific
position. This precise spot is known to
shamans as the *place of no pity*.

There really is no procedure involved in making the assemblage point move to the place of no pity. The spirit touches the person and his assemblage point moves. It is as simple as that.

What we need to do to allow magic to get hold of us is to banish doubts from our minds. Once doubts are banished, anything is possible.

Man's possibilities are so vast and
mysterious that warriors, rather than
thinking about them, have chosen to
explore them, with no hope of ever
understanding them.

Everything that warriors do is done as a consequence of a movement of their assemblage points, and such movements are ruled by the amount of energy warriors have at their command.

Any movement of the assemblage point means a movement away from an excessive concern with the individual self. Shamans believe it is the position of the assemblage point which makes modern man a homicidal egotist, a being totally involved with his self-image. Having lost hope of ever returning to the source of everything, the average man seeks solace in his selfishness.

The thrust of the warriors' way is to dethrone self-importance. And everything warriors do is directed toward accomplishing this goal.

Shamans have unmasked self-importance and found that it is self-pity masquerading as something else.

In the world of everyday life, one's word or one's decisions can be reversed very easily. The only irrevocable thing in the everyday world is death. In the shamans' world, on the other hand, normal death can be countermanded, but not the shamans' word. In the shamans' world decisions cannot be changed or revised. Once they have been made, they stand forever.

One of the most dramatic things about the human condition is the macabre connection between stupidity and self-reflection. It is stupidity that forces the average man to discard anything that does not conform with his self-reflective expectations. For example, as average men, we are blind to the most crucial piece of knowledge available to a human being: the existence of the assemblage point and the fact that it can move.

For the rational man to hold stead-
fastly to his self-image ensures his
abysmal ignorance. He ignores the fact
that shamanism is not incantations and
hocus-pocus, but the freedom to perceive
not only the world taken for granted, but
everything else that is humanly possible to accomplish. He trembles at the
possibility of freedom. And freedom is at
his fingertips.

Man's predicament is that he intuits his hidden resources, but he does not dare use them. This is why warriors say that man's plight is the counterpoint between his stupidity and his ignorance. Man needs now, more than ever, to be taught new ideas that have to do exclusively with his inner world—shamans' ideas, not social ideas, ideas pertaining to man facing the unknown, facing his personal death. Now, more than anything else, he needs to be taught the secrets of the assemblage point.

The spirit listens only when the speaker speaks in gestures. And gestures do not mean signs or body movements, but acts of true abandon, acts of largesse, of humor. As a gesture for the spirit, warriors bring out the best of themselves and silently offer it to the abstract.

Commentary

The last book that I ever wrote about don Juan as a direct result of the guidance of Florinda Matus was called *The Power of Silence*, a title that was chosen by my editor; my title had been *Inner Silence*. At the time that I was working on the book, the views of the shamans of ancient Mexico had become extremely abstract for me. Florinda tried her best to deviate me from my absorption in the abstract. She attempted to redirect my attention to different aspects of old shamanistic techniques, or she tried to divert me by shocking me with her scandalous behavior. But nothing was sufficient to deviate me from my seemingly inexorable drive.

The Power of Silence is an intellectual review of the thoughts of the shamans of ancient Mexico, in their most abstract guise. As I worked alone on the book, I was contaminated by the mood of those men, by their desire to know more in a quasi-rational way. Florinda explained that in the end, those shamans had become extremely cold and detached. Nothing warm existed for them anymore. They were set in their quest: their coldness as men was an effort to match the coldness of infinity. They had succeeded in changing their human eyes to match the cold eyes of the unknown.

I sensed this in myself, and tried desperately to turn the tide. I haven't succeeded yet. My thoughts have become more and more like the thoughts of those men at the end of their quest. It is not that I don't laugh. Quite the contrary, my life is an endless joy. But at the same time, it is an endless, merciless quest. Infinity will swallow me, and I want to be prepared for it. I don't want infinity to dissolve me into nothing because I hold human desires, warm affection, attachments, no matter how vague. More than anything else in this world, I want to be like those men. I never knew them. The only shamans I knew were don Juan and his cohorts, and what they expressed was the furthest thing from the coldness that I intuit in those unknown men.

Due to the influence that Florinda had on my life, I succeeded brilliantly in learning to focus my unwavering attention on the mood of people I never knew. I focused my recapitulation attention on the mood of those shamans, and I got trapped by it without hope of ever extricating myself from their pull. Florinda didn't believe in the finality of my state. She humored me, and laughed at it openly.

"Your state only seems to be final," she said to me, "but it isn't. A moment will come when you will change venues. Perhaps you will chuck every thought about the shamans of ancient Mexico. Perhaps you may even chuck the thoughts and views of the very shamans you worked with so closely, like the nagual Juan Matus. You might refuse his being. You'll see. The warrior has no limits. His sense of improvisation is so acute that he will make constructs out of nothing, but not just mere empty constructs; rather, something workable, pragmatic. You'll see. It is not that you'll forget about them, but at one moment, before you plunge into the abyss, if you have the gall to walk along its edge, if you have the daring not to deviate from it, you will then arrive at warriors' conclusions of an order and stability infinitely more suited to you than the fixation of the shamans of ancient Mexico."

Florinda's words were like a handsome, hopeful prophecy. Perhaps she was right. She was of course right in asserting that the resources of a warrior have no limits. The only flaw is that in order for me to have a different orderly view of the world and myself, a view even more suited to my temperament, I have to walk along the edge of the abyss, and I have doubts that I have the daring and strength to accomplish that feat.

But who is there to tell?